The Simple Guide to Collective Trauma

also in the Simple Guides *series*

The Simple Guide to Child Trauma
What It Is and How to Help
Betsy de Thierry
Illustrated by Emma Reeves
Foreword by David Shemmings
ISBN 978 1 78592 136 0
eISBN 978 1 78450 401 4

The Simple Guide to Sensitive Boys
How to Nurture Children and Avoid Trauma
Betsy de Thierry
Illustrated by Emma Reeves
Foreword by Jane Evans
ISBN 978 1 78592 325 8
eISBN 978 1 78450 639 1

The Simple Guide to Understanding Shame in Children
What It Is, What Helps and How to Prevent Further Stress or Trauma
Betsy de Thierry
Illustrated by Emma Reeves
Foreword by Dr Marc Bush
ISBN 978 1 78592 505 4
eISBN 978 1 78450 895 1

The Simple Guide to Attachment Difficulties in Children
What They Are and How to Help
Betsy de Thierry
Illustrated by Emma Reeves
Foreword by Carrie Grant
ISBN 978 1 78592 639 6
eISBN 978 1 78592 640 2

The Simple Guide to Complex Trauma and Dissociation
What It Is and How to Help
Betsy de Thierry
Illustrated by Emma Reeves
Foreword by Graham Music
ISBN 978 1 78775 314 3
eISBN 978 1 78775 315 0

The
Simple Guide to
Collective Trauma

What It Is, How It Affects Us and How to Help

Betsy de Thierry

Foreword by Lisa Cherry

Illustrated by Emma Reeves

Jessica Kingsley Publishers
London and Philadelphia

First published in Great Britain in 2021 by Jessica Kingsley Publishers
An Hachette Company

3

Copyright © Betsy de Thierry 2021
Illustrations copyright © Emma Reeves 2021
Foreword copyright © Lisa Cherry 2021

Front cover image source: Emma Reeves.

A CIP catalogue record for this title is available from the
British Library and the Library of Congress

ISBN 978 1 78775 788 2
eISBN 978 1 78775 789 9

Printed and bound by CPI Group (UK) Ltd, Croydon, CR0 4YY

Jessica Kingsley Publishers' policy is to use papers that are natural,
renewable and recyclable products and made from wood grown in
sustainable forests. The logging and manufacturing processes are expected
to conform to the environmental regulations of the country of origin.

Jessica Kingsley Publishers
Carmelite House
50 Victoria Embankment
London EC4Y 0DZ

www.jkp.com

CONTENTS

FOREWORD

The challenge of making simple the complexity of trauma is not lost on Betsy. All her 'Simple Guides' aim to open up a deeper, more coherent conversation and this book on collective trauma is no exception. Her very ability to give any kind of manageable definition to 'collective trauma' is what makes this book so important and offers the reader an anchor upon which to continue the exploration.

> Collective and community trauma is the reaction to an event or period of time where people share a traumatic experience whilst feeling terror, powerlessness and overwhelm. Whilst the collective trauma may be shared, the people will have varied experiences of it and will respond to these experiences differently, depending on their own personal backgrounds and current context.

Any writing about trauma challenges the writer *and* the reader as we go within, drawing upon the experiences that we may have had during our lives. Some of those experiences may sit so far within our bodies that we can almost pretend that they are not there. It is from this place that we might choose what we read and what we don't read; our bodies tell us that we do indeed know what we carry. It is worth being aware of those sensations in the body as you read, devouring their wisdom as they tell you that which it can be hard to tell ourselves in words. Be kind to yourself; collective trauma is all around us and Betsy offers examples of her own experience to gently take us on this internal exploration.

Betsy cleverly explores relationships, recovery and healing and invites the reader to explore all these ideas through reflective questions at the end of each chapter. In doing so, she reminds us that sleep, safety, breath, play and art support us in our healing. It is vital that we understand that we can recover. We *do* recover. But we will always need each other to do so.

Lisa Cherry
speaker, trainer and author on
trauma, recovery and resilience

INTRODUCTION

This book is a simple guide to a large and emotive subject.

Collective trauma can impact a whole community and the impact can then subsequently echo through many generations.

The aim of this book, as with others in the 'Simple Guides' series, is not to provide a comprehensive account, but to help you to quickly gain an understanding of what collective trauma is, some common themes and characteristics, and how we can avoid the experience damaging our communities and generations to come.

This book aims to help anyone helping children or young people to recover from collective trauma. It also aims to equip the adult with knowledge that can facilitate change and hope for them and the younger generation. It also aims to equip the adult reader to help other adults, on the basis that all of us impact each other and if we can all build resilience and recover, then our communities will become healthier for all of us.

Although I specialise in developmental and complex trauma in my work, in my personal life, I am passionate about the overlap of every kind of trauma to humankind, and the ability to see how knowledge can positively impact whole communities.

Many readers of this book will have an experience of collective trauma; I have my own.

- **It can affect nations.** I was born into the Burundian genocide in 1972 which left a continual sense of underlying tension and anxiety in the air of the beautiful country that I love. It is in nations like this that we see clearly how such atrocities have impacted multiple generations. Shock, terror, loss and bereavement have impacted everyone over the years.

- **It can affect organisations.** On a far less traumatic scale, when I had a death threat and subsequent harassment and stalking in the UK, the people within the organisations that I led were impacted due to my inability to feel like I could be a part of the city where I lived. It became an experience of collective trauma, although many chose to leave the organisations quickly to avoid becoming traumatised, for fear that they would also be targeted.

- **It affects individuals.** The five years of horror I faced as part of the stalking and harassment are very much part of my personal story and now also part of the story of the organisations I have been leading. Whilst some people left the organisations due to the volatility it caused, others stayed, and we made sure that post-traumatic growth was intentional. For me personally, I had to process my own pain to be able to continue to lead organisations that help others through trauma.

Collective trauma can affect individuals, organisations and nations and yet the impact can be wider still. This is shown by the important awakening of a generation to the extent of racism, prejudice and discrimination that has been tolerated for far too long.

Whilst my experience in Burundi was primarily about the horrors of community hatred and murder, my experience in the UK was about the power of words being used to try to destroy lives.

An understanding of trauma can diminish the impact of destructive experiences and can even facilitate post-traumatic growth. I hope that this book helps you as you make a difference to those around you in the way you choose to use your words, your skills, your choices and your ability to love others despite pain.

The fact that you are reading this means that you are already committed to being intentional about changing lives and for that I salute you! If no one has ever said it to you before – well done and thank you for not sinking into a self-absorbed bubble of denial, but instead continuing to learn and help others – whether that's your loved ones or a whole community, organisation or nation.

Well done!

Betsy x

Chapter One

AN INTRODUCTION TO COLLECTIVE TRAUMA AND THE IMPACT OF THE THREAT RESPONSE

What is collective trauma?

Let's start with the definition of the word trauma. Trauma can be defined as any experience or repeated experience where the person feels terrified, powerless and overwhelmed, to the extent that it challenges their capacity to cope. It can leave an imprint on the person's nervous system, emotions, body, behaviours, learning and relationships.

There are so many different traumatic experiences and it's important to explore what themes they have in common and where the impact of them differs. Most of my clinical work is focused on developmental trauma and interpersonal trauma, such as abuse, neglect and attachment trauma – where the child was terrified, powerless and overwhelmed over a sustained period of time.

I often refer to the trauma continuum (de Thierry 2015), which gives us language around the different impacts of those experiences. Type I trauma is described as a single traumatic incident whilst Type II trauma is described as multiple, repeated traumatic experiences over a length of time. Type III trauma is a name which attempts to capture a description of a life full of repeated, severe, multiple and different traumatic experiences.

The term PTSD (post-traumatic stress disorder) is not used in the book because the symptoms of trauma are seen as just that – behaviours that demonstrate that the person has been impacted by the traumatic experience. I do not believe we need to frame these coping mechanisms as a disorder.

There are other traumatic experiences which share the same theme of terror, powerlessness and loss. Some traumatic experiences are due to politics, wars or genocides or major large-scale events like **a pandemic or natural disaster**.

Other traumatic experiences, for example relating to identity, race or culture, can be continual and destructive, but they can often be overlooked or misunderstood. This can be because of a sense of shame that causes them to be pushed aside or hidden from public attention to avoid further rejection or misunderstanding, but these experiences also need to be understood and validated.

Of course, we know that there is multigenerational trauma, caused by experiences such as poverty or community violence, where there has been suffering for many centuries.

There is the experience of sibling and peer trauma – often called bullying – school trauma, medical trauma, organisational trauma and of course the trauma caused by natural disasters.

This is not a comprehensive list but it should be sufficient to show that the world of trauma recovery is broad and complex!

Collective and community trauma, the subject of this book, are reactions to an event or period of time where people share a traumatic experience whilst feeling terror, powerlessness and overwhelm. Whilst we sometimes use the terms collective trauma and community trauma interchangeably, the term community trauma points more to a traumatic experience that impacts and shatters the sense of norm in a group of people who spend time together, whereas collective trauma is the shattering of lives who share something that defines them, regardless of if they had been an active part of the community before the traumatic experience.

Whilst the collective trauma is shared, people will have varied experiences of it and will respond to these experiences differently, depending on their own personal backgrounds and current context.

This book will explore the impact of collective trauma on children and young people but also on adults, because the impact on the adults has a direct effect on the younger generation. Sometimes I will refer to the impact on 'people', because it is similar for both children and adults.

Collective trauma can impact us all, but not all of us are traumatised by events and experiences which are traumatic for others. Some people may experience stress or a crisis, but it doesn't have to cause long-term traumatic impact. Usually, the degree of traumatic impact of any terrifying experience is connected to the child's ability to find comfort and reassurance from a safe and known adult, both in the immediate aftermath of the experience and then as a safe place to further explore the experience over time (de Thierry 2019).

Many children are unable to find that emotional connection and comforting safe place with their key adult. This can be for different reasons – the adult being unavailable, the adult being overwhelmed with their own terror, or threats or fear of what may happen to either of them. A trauma recovery-focused culture is one where we recognise that we can't make assumptions and we will never shame or blame anyone, because we don't know what was going on for them.

It is important to also acknowledge that any collective trauma experience can exacerbate pre-existing trauma symptoms that are present due to previous experiences of trauma. These symptoms can become further escalated if the person feels less safe and out of control and their normality has been disrupted. We will explore the impact of collective trauma on normal life in Chapter 4.

Collective trauma can be caused by events such as:

- war

- natural disasters such as tsunamis, fires, floods, etc.

- mass shootings or public violence

- genocides

- pandemics

- terrorist attacks

- economic disasters

- any other one-off traumatic event which is witnessed by a collective of people

- a continual traumatic repeated event, which is on-going, with ongoing impact and shock.

This list is not exhaustive because there are many different types of collective trauma. Some are immediate and sudden. Others are less immediately dramatic, but last longer, such as a pandemic, economic crisis, or community 'unrest'. Sometimes these events are witnessed first-hand, but they may also be observed through the media.

For example, the tragedy of 9/11 was a traumatic event that was witnessed by many people on their televisions across the world, whilst being experienced first-hand by thousands of people on the ground, with relatives and friends across the USA and further afield feeling worried about if their friends and loved ones had been hurt or had not survived.

Collective trauma can cause huge shock and a sense of the community being changed suddenly. It often raises new questions and creates concerns about the future.

Collective trauma and the impact on the whole community

One way that collective trauma can have a strong impact on the community is when there is a slow realisation that the community has changed around the traumatic experience, and people have had to make dysfunctional adaptations to cope, now that the everything that 'was' seems to have changed considerably.

Erikson (1986) describes it powerfully as a:

> blow to the basic tissues of social life that damages the bonds attaching people together and impairs the prevailing sense of community. The collective trauma works its way slowly and even insidiously into the awareness of those who suffer from it, so it doesn't have the quality of suddenness normally associated with 'trauma'. But it is a form of shock all the same, a gradual realisation that the community no longer exists as an effective source of support and that an important part of the self has disappeared... (p.154)

Collective trauma and relationships

We often refer to relational trauma when we think about experiences that have a terrifying element within a relationship, such as domestic violence, abuse and assault. These traumatic experiences are the focus of several of my other 'Simple Guides' books, which explore the trauma symptoms that arise due to the terror, powerlessness and overwhelm that is a central experience in such trauma and which can lead to further difficulties with trust and vulnerability. Collective trauma can, however, also share some of the same damage to relationships because it immediately impacts people at the core of their sense of safety and predictability and control over their life. Those who experience collective trauma may feel betrayed by those who should or could help them feel safe, and that could be individual people or organisations. Collective trauma causes disruptions of relationships at all levels of human systems and so therefore there needs to be some kind of collective recovery. Jack Saul is a psychologist who has created a number of programmes for populations in New York City who have experienced trauma. He explains that 'recovery then involves collective processes of readjustment and adaptation and the mobilization of capacities for resilience in families and communities' (Saul 2014, p.6).

Individual trauma can cause the person impacted – whether a child, young person or adult – to reel in shock, turmoil, pain and confusion about the world, their identity and place within it. In collective trauma, the person can also question the very fabric of their community, culture, nation or world and their place within it. A more innocent view of the world has been suddenly stolen from them and it can seem that things will never be the same ever again.

Relationships, however, can be strengthened in collective trauma as people recognise their shared experience and support each other. This sense of belonging can facilitate the establishment of shared safe places, a strengthened cultural identity and stronger communities.

The impact of trauma on the brain and behaviour

In times of collective trauma, children and young people learn instinctively that the world is not as safe as they had thought.

For many, their innocence – the idea that nothing bad would happen to them and their safe adults would protect them – has been shattered. We have to explain any potential dangers to them, warning them of the possibility that further bad things could happen. It is no surprise when we realise that their little bodies are then full of nervousness about their world and what will happen next. We know that when children, young people or adults feel fear we have a biological, instinctive reaction that energises the part of our brain that is designed to keep us safe and this then causes less neural activity in other regions of the brain.

People's fight, flight and freeze responses become dominant as the fear makes their survival brain take over and prepare for threat. When their bodies are on high alert, waiting for a threat to take place, they can struggle to rest, be calm or learn anything that may distract them from this state of being 'alert for danger'. We call this hypervigilance. It also makes them easily distracted and ready to fight if there is any sound of danger! Their bodies are pumped with cortisol and adrenaline so that they are ready for fight or flight, but this eventually makes them feel ill, grumpy and tired. Children show us that they are trying to manage these big feelings and stress hormones in their behaviours, and that's why we often say 'all behaviour is communication'.

Those children who have trauma before may know that fighting and running aren't always successful and so they freeze and become withdrawn, seem to be in another world in their head, or try to be invisible to others. When they have to cope with changes to their familiar routine, futures that are unpredictable, collective stress, fear, loss or empathising with others who are in grief and loss, it can all be too much for them.

This feeling of it all being 'too much' can then lead many people to want to be in denial, suppress negative emotions or focus on only cheering others up to distract from feeling their own pain. However, being aware of our own pain, fear, helplessness and overwhelm is immensely difficult but something that is important and best done with others. Feeling our difficult feelings is important to the recovery from collective trauma.

Recovery from collective trauma

Is recovery possible? What does recovery look like? These are good questions that it would be worthwhile for us all to reflect on. What we do know is that when people have experienced collective trauma, they may never be the same again, but that is not necessary unequivocally bad. They may learn about the fragility of life, the importance of spending time with and appreciating those they love; they may have a light bulb moment that material gain is not the thing that matters in life and slowing down to appreciate the small things can be transformative.

There can be a strengthening of identity, community relationships and families. As communities search for meaning, they can often find hope and a positive future. Towards the end of the book, we will even explore the possibility of post-traumatic growth. Recovery is possible – but it may not look like we imagine…

Reflection points

- How have you been impacted by collective trauma?

- How has this collective trauma impacted your experience of community?

- What sort of areas of our life can be impacted by collective trauma?

Chapter Two

THE POWER OF RELATIONSHIPS

Relationships

Relationships are a central theme within our understanding of how to recover from trauma.

We often say that when we have been hurt in a relationship or through relationships, we heal best within healthy relationships. As humans we need others to help us live life. We start off life fully dependent on adults to feed, clothe and care for us, and in our early years we also develop an understanding of the world and who we are within it from those who care for us. Our sense of identity is formed through interactions with those around us, and our response to those. As we go through life as a baby, toddler, child, teenager and adult we depend on others for fun, laughter, comfort, company, stimulation, a sense of belonging and a sense of being fully alive. Bessel van der Kolk (2014) sums it up by saying that 'our capacity to destroy one another is matched by our capacity to heal one another' (p.38).

Loneliness and isolation

Loneliness and isolation are bad for us and yet often when people are struggling the most others can have a tendency to withdraw from them, often 'in case they make it worse'. This sense of being alone in a traumatic time, which brings with it a natural sense of aloneness, can be detrimental. Psychologist Dr Loardes (quoted in Young 2020) says in her research into the impact of isolation during the coronavirus pandemic, 'From our analysis, it is clear there are strong associations between loneliness and depression in young people, both in the immediate and the longer term.' She explains that the duration of loneliness seems to have the biggest negative impact and the sooner that they can start having regular, normal connection with others the better. Facilitating positive relationships can change the life of a child, young person or adult and can also bring about healing.

We know that our brain is a living system that continually absorbs and processes information and is always changing. Louis Cozolino, an American psychologist and writer, explains the powerful fact about the impact of isolation in brain development:

> Neurons are, by their nature social; they shun isolation and depend on their neighbours for survival. If they aren't sending and receiving messages from their other neurons on a constant basis, they literally shrink and die. (2006, p.36)

The following excerpt is from my previous book *The Simple Guide to Attachment Difficulties* (2019).

Oxytocin: Our social connectedness hormone

A baby in the womb is designed to experience oxytocin whilst growing, as the mum strokes and chats to her unborn child as she waits for the birth. Oxytocin is a neurotransmitter (chemical substance that sends messages) and a hormone that is produced in the hypothalamus (the small but important centre in the brain which helps with hormone production and other things), where it is then transported to and secreted from the pituitary gland (master gland) at the base of the brain.

It is often called the 'love chemical' or 'attachment hormone' because it is released during hugging, childbirth or when two people are experiencing emotional connection. If oxytocin wasn't naturally produced in childbirth, I suspect there would be significantly fewer births due to the level of pain! The hormone causes 'happy highs' that enable the mums to 'fall in love' with their child rather than resent them for the pain endured.

Ideally, at the birth, the mum is able to immediately greet her baby with relief because both the mum and baby are flooded with oxytocin leading to the baby feeling safe and the mum feeling elated. The mum may have been deeply stressed and terrified by the birthing experience, but the oxytocin enables there to be joy at the birth. It is in her arms that a baby should begin the journey of learning that stress and fear is tolerable because she will then comfort them and make them feel safe. This leads to the mum being the primary attachment figure and therefore the source of safety and comfort.

Social relationships

Oxytocin continues to be an important hormone that is released when the baby and then toddler and child are comforted or laugh or share pleasure together.

The orbitofrontal cortex area of the brain is busy dealing with emotional responses and behaviours that are located in the subconscious, and is the centre of social relationships. The prefrontal cortex is like the control centre for the other regions of the brain that hold emotional reactions and impulses; it is a part of the brain that only develops after birth and only in the context of relationships.

Researchers would describe it as 'experience dependent'. The continuous and repetitive co-regulation between a parent or carer and the baby or toddler helps them lay down patterns which naturally develop into self-regulation of their emotions and reactions. These experiences are full of oxytocin release and develop the orbitofrontal cortex. (de Thierry 2019, pp.35–38)

Oxytocin is a hormone that is critical in human life for a lot of reasons. There can be a release of oxytocin during any kind of safe, social contact, not just between family members, and it can cause a sense of calmness and joy.

When oxytocin is not there, depression, hopelessness and lack of sense of purpose can bubble to the surface. Any collective trauma that causes isolation and a breakdown in community experiences can be significantly detrimental to the mental health of those within it.

Suffer together: Heal together

Humans develop a sense of identity though the traditions, beliefs and culture around them. What is 'normal' around us becomes normal to us. In the generations before us or cultures that may not be familiar to us, there are some excellent practices that demonstrate how we can best heal our communities after collective trauma. We will explore some of them in this chapter.

There are certain characteristics that we need to learn about and re-create as normal in our cultures, because they enable healing and recovery from collective trauma, such as the use of singing and storytelling. For many of us, our current cultures actually foster denial, isolation, repression and de-validating the traumatic experiences.

When we hurt and feel pain, we can feel better when someone around us can show authentic empathy and compassion. This reduces the physical pain and emotional pain. Although our words can rarely contain and describe much of our feelings about our human frailty, confusion and suffering, it is powerful to be properly heard when we try to use them. Within the therapy world we use the phrase 'empathetic witness' as an essential element of our role in supporting people who need to unpack, process and make sense of the horrors that they have experienced. We can choose to be an empathetic listener by taking an active listening posture with our bodies – leaning in, caring, with facial expressions that are showing empathy and can mirror some of the other person's expressions so that people can feel heard. When they feel heard, people feel valued and cared for and loved. This sense of being valued and belonging to a group of others begins to heal the turmoil of trauma and the shock of loss. Conversely, when we suffer in isolation and others around us seem preoccupied and they don't offer validation and comfort, the sense of aloneness is escalated and the pain worsens as it is pushed, unwanted, into the dark crevices of the subconscious.

As has been mentioned, talking about loss and trauma is very difficult and can even be re-traumatising, and so a preferable approach that can facilitate recovery and help with some kind of reduction in pain is more practical and creative, but involves the whole community understanding the power of empathy and kindness. To grasp some of the approaches that work, we can look at cultures that embrace grief, loss and pain as a part of being alive.

Bruce Perry speaks of some different cultures that show us how to build stronger, healthier communities. He describes how they share common elements in their traditions which:

> include an overarching belief system – a rationale, a belief, a reason for the pain, injury, loss, a re-telling or re-enactment of the trauma in words, dance, or a song; a set of somato-sensory experiences – touch, the patterned repetitive movements of dance, and song – all provided in an intensely relational experience with family and clan participating in the ritual. (Foreword to Malchiodi 2008, p.x)

We know that these activities stimulate different parts of the brain and so healing can begin in all those areas that are impacted by the terror. Perry suggests (in Malchiodi 2008)

some activities that seem to build authentic community, whilst facilitating collective healing. These activities are 'normal' in some cultures and seen as central to every day community life. They include experiences such as re-telling the story, dancing, singing, and using drama to re-tell the story. Other sensory experiences that help to rebuild communities are creative projects such as sculpture, music and creating images of the experiences. Of course, anything that helps people to connect to others to facilitate a sense of community and belonging can be healing: eating together, hugs and any gatherings.

I would add to the list:

- facilitating joint, shared creative projects

- rebuilding/painting/helping together in community investment projects

- facilitating shared rhythm activities such as drumming, choirs, clapping circles

- finding ways of telling the stories for generations to come

- sharing food in large groups who have been through the same traumatic experience.

Music can be a powerful way of creating a sense of belonging without the intensity of focusing on the shared traumatic experience, and can be healing for many reasons. Stephen Porges speaks of music as a method that 'has been used to calm, to enable feelings of safety, to build a sense of community, and to reduce the social distance between people' (2011, p.246).

Conclusion

We need to recognise the centrality of relationships within the healing and recovery process of collective trauma. We know that when we can facilitate any kind of community experiences that are based on kindness, empathy, listening and validation of emotions, we can see the community heal and the people within that community heal. There have been thousands of generations of people who have found their communities have recovered from horrific experiences because of these foundational principles.

Reflection points

- Which relationship had a positive impact on you as a child?

- Do you have a sense of belonging to a larger group? Why?

- What activities could you facilitate to enable others around you to heal?

Chapter Three

THE CENTRALITY OF SAFETY

The importance of safety is as much a central theme within trauma recovery as the importance of relationships. The overwhelming terror of trauma cannot even begin to subside, even long after the event, if the child is unable to feel safe. Dr Stephen Porges (2011) speaks about the centrality of safety within the work of trauma recovery and how that impacts our emotions, nervous systems and behaviour. When a child has experienced a traumatic event, they urgently need to find physical and emotional safety away from the terror, with some kind of comfort and someone to care for them and protect them. For some children they can then immediately feel the relief of safety, but others, for whom the traumatic experience has been relentless or too shocking, may not be able to feel safe for a long time, even if they are actually safe.

Safety is interconnected with attachment relationships

The first work is to help the child find physical safety with a home, food and their basic needs met. Then we recognise that safety is found in their primary relationships, which we could call their attachment relationships. The following definition of the primary attachment relationship of parent or carer is from my book, *The Simple Guide to Attachment Difficulties*, which explores the subject at length:

> Attachment is the specific element of parenting that goes beyond the physical needs of the child being met and speaks of the emotional availability of the child's primary caregiver to be an emotional safety regulator for the child. (de Thierry 2019, p.18)

When the primary caregiver is able to be emotionally available to the child and make time to connect emotionally, the child can feel safe, known, understood, cared for and their emotions can be explored and validated. This is the main way children feel safe; it starts with a relationship where they feel protected, nurtured and loved. If the child has either not experienced the consistent care and emotional connection of a primary caregiver, or if they have lost their safe adult due to tragedy, then safety will be much harder to find and will require other adults stepping into the shoes of a primary caregiver, whilst also knowing they will need to offer consistent care over a long period of time.

Safety is almost impossible when there are multiple adults trying to help a child, but each one is only involved for a short period of time. The constant changes can leave the child feeling confused and unsafe. An adult who is able to offer an attachment relationship where they can provide longer-term commitment, care and emotional connection can change the life and trajectory of the child because they can potentially become a safe place and safe relationship. If we feel safe relationally, we often then feel safe emotionally and then our bodies can relax. Bessel van der Kolk (2014) describes the centrality of safety in our relationships leading to healthy lives; 'more than anything else, being able to feel safe with other people defines mental health; safe connections are fundamental to meaningful and satisfying lives' (p.352).

How feeling unsafe can limit life

We know that when humans feel safe, we can laugh, think, create and be vulnerable, which leads to stronger relationships. We also know that when we are in a survival state the neural activity is primarily found in the brainstem (primitive, automatic) and limbic (relational, emotional) area of the brain, which means that there is significantly less neural activity in the prefrontal cortex where thinking, reflection, empathy, negotiation, imagination and creativity take place. Fear can cause us to be more comfortable with a daily routine that requires little cognitive effort and can be achieved with instinctive automatic behaviour, because our brain can be taken up with trying to survive.

Listening empathetically

Listening is a skill that can create extraordinary change in our communities when it is understood as a gift that we can give to others. When we give children, young people and their adults the space and time to talk or just 'be' with us that sense of being understood and valued can begin to help them learn to trust again. I like to picture a tortoise hiding under the shell, but when we listen, the head pokes out to see if we are trustworthy! At that point, although there is nervousness about being rejected or frightened further, if the person feels that we authentically care, then they can let themselves be seen. In our world that seems to be dominated by spreadsheets, data and testing, sometimes it can be healing for children and young people to know that there are people who care – just because – and not so that they can tweet the experience or use the time spent as evidence for anything!

Physical and practical aspects of safety

The spaces that we use to interact with children and young people need to be thought through to ensure they are places that feel safe. The child will make an instinctive decision about the space immediately and so obvious visual indicators of comfort and fun need to be seen easily. Thought needs to go into the small aspects so that each child feels welcome and thought about, for example with toys or books about children representing different cultures and races. The spaces we offer children and young people to come and explore their challenges and pain need to be creative yet calm; warm and yet professional; comforting and inspiring. As we offer 'safe spaces' in the physical, the children will be able to find their safe spaces internally. The following passage is an extract from my previous book, *The Simple Guide to Complex Trauma and Dissociation*. I have reproduced it here because it is so important that we understand how the brain may respond to perceived threats and the importance of feeling safe.

A child will be continually evaluating their safety and any possible dangers. Porges (2017) uses the word 'neuroception' to explain the way that our nervous system evaluates safety and danger. It is an automatic, primitive, instinctive process where our own nervous system assesses the safety or risk around us and then instinctively reacts as a result of the evaluation. For example, if we have experienced a house fire and we go to a friend's house for fireworks night and we are picturing fireworks in our imagination but as we arrive we smell fire, our neuroception could suggest that we are not safe and make a run from the house despite our cognitive brain knowing it will probably be a bonfire. Or if Becky goes to a friend's house and they all start to make hot chocolate, Becky may suddenly say that she is going home and pretend she has homework to do. It could be that she suddenly panics and knows she has to run because her subconscious remembers that she was always given hot chocolate before she was abused. Although she doesn't make the connection when her friends suggest it, her body knows and makes her want to run. It could be a tiny trigger such as a raised eyebrow, or a smell or any sensory trigger that alerts the nervous system to tell us that we aren't safe. Children assess if it's the best time to talk to their parents or carers about something they did wrong by looking at their face, their body posture and getting a 'feel' for whether it's a good time or not. Sadly, some of us adults can have a nervous system that is stuck in overwhelm due to our experience of life or we are just constantly busy or anxious, and so when we say with our words 'you can always talk to me about anything' our 'vibe' or our nervous system can seem to contradict that and so the child doesn't feel like they can tell us important things. That's why it is important to be aware of our own nervous system and our own sense of wellbeing and work on our own anxiety so that we offer calm, grounded, safe adult care.

Porges' Polyvagal theory presents our physiological nervous system as being in three parts, like a traffic light; we move from one state to another all the time. We are either in a relaxed social state, which is like the green colour of the traffic light and is called 'the social engagement system'. If we feel nervous or threatened, then we immediately activate our sympathetic nervous system, which alerts our body to respond to danger. This is our 'primitive threat response', where we feel threatened – a fight, flight or freeze response. It is like the amber warning traffic light. The third state is called 'the dorsal vagal state', where we are now terrified and believe there is a danger to life, so we shut down or we dissociate. It is neuroception that moves us from one state or colour to the other, according to what we notice in our environment that makes us feel calm and safe or panicky and frightened. It's not a bad thing moving into the sympathetic nervous system short term, because that can give us extra energy and confidence if we feel nervous or anxious; but we don't want to stay there. It is hoped the people around us will help us feel safe with their facial reactions and tone of voice and we will move into the safe and social engagement system. Human connection enables us to feel safe and facilitates healing. (de Thierry 2020, pp.90–93)

What can we do to help the child feel safe?

There are activities and sensory tools that can be used to help a child feel safer in the context of offering a warm and empathetic relationship. Dr Bessel van der Kolk (2014) explains how important it is to feel safe. He says, 'The single most important issue for traumatised people is to find a sense of safety in their own bodies.'

One popular method of helping a child, young person or adult to move from a stressed and panicky state to a calmer state is called grounding. It is easy to learn to help to 'ground' someone by using certain words and approaches.

We can be warm, genuinely caring and approach the stressed person asking if we can help. We can use words to signal safety verbally such as: 'It's okay'; 'You're okay'; 'You're safe here'; 'I'm with you'; 'I can see you seem stressed'; 'This is really hard'.

We can help them bring their prefrontal cortex back into a place where they can think and reflect again by saying things that help to label the experience they may be having. For example: 'I don't think you're fully here with me'; 'Can you tell me what's going on for you?'; 'Tell me what's happening right now?'; 'Can you look around and see where you are?'

We can also help them find sensory comforts such as objects that smell comforting or have a texture that feels comforting, or a space where they feel safe.

What can we do to help the adult feel safe?

In a similar way to children, the adult who is caring for the child needs to feel safe themselves. We know that when the adults are stressed and traumatised, their nervous system responds and the child can pick that up and can sense their anxiety and feel more unsafe. We need to make sure the adults look after themselves and have people who care for them too. The adults can also be taught to find sensory things that can help them feel safe, such as things that they can smell, things they can touch, places they can go to which help them feel calm, beautiful places and relaxing places – even if it's for just a few minutes. It is important for the adult to explore what helps them feel safe and have some time to reflect, process, cry or be.

Reflection points

- What sensory things make you feel safe? How about those you care for?

- Have you felt better when you have been listened to and validated?

- Have you tried using grounding as a way of becoming safe emotionally in the here and now?

Chapter Four

THE IMPACT OF COLLECTIVE TRAUMA ON NORMAL LIFE

The experience of collective trauma can have an extraordinary impact on our daily life and it can often become clear that even areas of life that seemed unrelated to the trauma have subtle signs of being impacted. This chapter will explore a few of the different ways that collective trauma can impact the day to day, normal life of children.

Here are some of the behaviours that are common when a child is in shock, or has been very frightened or experienced collective trauma or any other kind of trauma:

- their behaviour is regressive – younger than their biological age

- they worry more about little things

- they struggle to sleep deeply or go to sleep

- they need more comfort

- they need more attention

- they are more tired

- they are more tearful

- they eat too much or don't want to eat

- they are more angry and irritable

- they feel numb or show fewer emotional responses

- they feel anxious and may be twitchy to sounds or smells

- they have tummy aches, headaches or other aches

- they have catastrophic thoughts that something awful will happen again

- they worry about their home, money, food, water, toys

- they feel 'survivor's guilt' for being better off than others

- they are less interested in things they used to be passionate about.

Hypervigilance

For any of us who have lived through a traumatic event or period of time, it becomes natural to try to feel prepared for another trauma. It is logical to assume that if we prepare better, we won't be so shocked the next time something horrific occurs. Obviously, this logic is dysfunctional and by the very nature of the issue, no amount of preparation can enable trauma to be less of a shock. However, this instinctual protective behaviour means that unless we have intentionally sought comfort and safety, we will probably feel unsafe on a primitive, subconscious level. If there is the possibility of more terror and powerlessness occurring, hypervigilance becomes normal.

Hypervigilance is a coping mechanism and a symptom of

trauma. It is when our brains stay on 'alert' for danger and we can become twitchier, responding to sounds, sights and smells with primitive survival speed, as if our lives depend on it. In a pandemic, when someone is heard sneezing or coughing, others around them tense up, curl up or if possible move away at speed. In areas where bombings, attacks and violence are frequent interruptions, any sudden noise, rumbling, shouting or even feelings of relational tension can cause a similar nervous reaction. No one knows when the next trauma will happen, so everyone remains ready to fight, flight or freeze at all times. This of course leads to increased tension in general, more sensitivities around sound, smell, feelings and sights, which lead to increased anxiety. Our world seems to be on edge.

Eventually, if you have lived like this for some time, another coping mechanism can kick into play due to this sense of overwhelm. Freeze is a way of surviving what seems like continual threat by almost becoming resigned to it. Lethargy can set in and exhaustion becomes the norm. On the other hand, sometimes people who have been traumatised seem to be at their best when there is another incident, crisis or trauma as they can rise to the occasion because they have in essence been waiting for this to happen, all their senses waiting to spring into action to help others and lead people through a disaster. Hypervigilance gives them the energy to spring into action quicker than many others and yet in other settings it can also mean that the same person may also be bored, irritable and struggle to relax when there are no signs of danger because they can't stop being on alert. This hypervigilance can impact every day and every experience within a day and it can be exhausting to live on alert for danger all the time.

Sleep

Sleep is a vital, restorative part of being human and yet the experience of trauma can impact the rhythm and routine of sleep. It is not abnormal for children to have nightmares, to be scared to go to sleep and need someone to be with them until they drop off, or for them to refuse to go to bed or be restless during their sleep.

Anxiety is a large reason that sleep is impacted and so the resolution to a good sleeping pattern would be to help the child feel safer and more comforted. As the previous chapter explored, there are ways of increasing sensory comfort, alongside the centrality of the child being reassured by their primary caregiver(s).

Practical tips for better sleep include trying to help the child to get enough exercise so that they are physically tired, which links to limited screen time as this can cause them to sit still and store nervous energy, instead of 'running it off'. Make sure they are not hungry or thirsty and have had enough time to talk and be listened to. We also know that routines are important, alongside having clear expectations of bedtimes and bedtime routines that have been talked through and agreed on with the child.

Learning and the impact of unnecessary information

If a child is in a survival state and on alert for the next danger that may invade their life, it is hard for them to focus on learning at school as the subject feels irrelevant to their survival. On the other hand, there are some children who want to focus on learning to distract them from their daily pain and loss, so they find comfort in throwing themselves into accumulating knowledge and learning which offer the possibility of success and achievement, both of which can decrease the sense of pain. These polarised possibilities of the impact of trauma on learning represent the reality of many different possible reactions to academic learning that we may see in the classroom following a collective trauma experience.

Anger and aggression

Anger is known as a bodyguard or guard dog emotion that hides sadness and fear. It acts as armour to protect vulnerability and powerlessness. Anger and aggression can escalate in times of collective trauma, because people can feel unsafe and rather than actually feel their own pain or fear, they would rather deflect from it to experience chaos. This defence mechanism can then spiral a group of people into fear and sadness which further stops them feeling safe and this can then cause the group to feel traumatised. Usually the angry person will take some time to feel safe enough to be able to be vulnerable, and safety can only be facilitated in the context of relationships where they feel valued, listened to and cared for. In this context, the outer shell of anger and self-defence can begin to melt, and they can begin to feel their pain, which leads them to need comfort and care. Children can only think through their angry behaviour once they have connected emotionally with a caring adult and therefore feel safe. Bruce Perry, a leading child psychiatrist in the field of trauma recovery, often refers to the sequence of calming down with the Three Rs: Regulate, Relate and Reason. There is no possibility of helping someone calm down if we start trying to reason with them first. We have to start at regulating with them, then relating (emotionally connecting) and then reasoning, once those two stages have been established.

Separation anxiety

It is obvious that when a child has experienced any kind of loss, they will be more nervous about any further impending loss. This means that they may struggle with separating physically from those who they love and find comfort from, which can lead to short-term or longer-term separation anxiety. This fear of separating can cause behaviours such as the child clinging to the adult, crying, screaming, shaking or total refusal to leave the adult they need. Or these feelings of fear can result in behaviours such as aggression, anger, violence and other physical demonstrations of the terror of the powerlessness that they are trying to avoid. There are no simple solutions to these behaviours, because the fear is usually grounded in some reality that the child has experienced, but there needs to be an approach which is based in kindness, patience, empathy and reassurance. We know that when we are annoyed, angry and impatient with the child, the separation anxiety just seems to get worse. The child needs to be helped with transitional objects – some kind of comforting thing that the loved one gives or lends to the child which helps them feel that they will come back to get the item, whilst also providing comfort from the smell or familiarity of the object. When the adult can explain clearly and gently give some expectations around the timings, activities and people who will be with them and when they can then see their adult, this can ease some of their worries. When the child sees their primary caregiver speaking and planning together with their teacher or helper about the child's safety, this can also reassure them that they are safe.

Sense of purpose and future

In a period of time when collective trauma has impacted an area or community, it does seem to be the case that some older children and young people can lose their energy and spark for life. They can feel a sense of hopelessness for the future because it is difficult to make plans when the infrastructure of society has changed. Our ability to have plans for positive experiences in the future is an essential element that brings hope, and when this is absent, depression and lethargy can set in. It is important to try to help them plan something positive, even if it seems small, because this helps them feel motivated for the present. Plans that can inspire them and spur them on usually involve the possibility of developing relationships or having a sense of belonging to a group.

On larger issues of life, we can see that many begin to struggle with meaning. Hirschberger (2018) says that 'collective trauma is a cataclysmic event that shatters the basic fabric of society. Aside from the horrific loss of life, collective trauma is also a crisis of meaning.'

Older children and young people may begin to have philosophical questions about the meaning of life, and if they are isolated, these thoughts can become dark and unhelpful, but if they are spoken about with others, can stimulate learning and curiosity.

Reflection points

- How has collective trauma impacted the daily life of those you care for?

- What behaviours have developed as a result of the collective trauma?

- What are the behaviours telling us about what the child needs right now?

Chapter Five

PARENTING AND SUPPORTING PARENTS AND CARERS

The centrality of parents and familiar carers to resilience and recovery

Often parents, carers and guardians can be overlooked when we think about how to enable children and young people to recover from a traumatic experience and yet we know that a child assesses their safety when they feel fear by looking immediately at their primary caregiver and their facial response. As a mum I have experienced different situations such as a sudden loud noise where my children immediately look at me with fear to check if they are safe. If I smile and reassure them, they relax and if I look frightened they cry with terror. If the adult looks calm and peaceful, the child assumes that whatever they saw was not as distressing as they may have first thought. If the face of the adult is distressed or terrified, then they have their fears confirmed and react accordingly. If a child sees a primary caregiver reacting with terror at something that others may subjectively believe is not of concern, such as thunder or dropping a plate, then the child learns that these are events to be afraid of.

We know that children react to their adults' non-verbal expressions far more than any words that may be used and so even if they use words such as 'It's fine!', if they are saying those words with a face that shows terror, then the child feels terror and is also confused! I remember a time I was about nine years old and was on holiday and in a cable car with my brother and parents. As it stopped midway, I hardly noticed it stop, but suddenly my mother started reciting prayers and looking deadly serious. The swinging of the cable car that I had found relaxing suddenly became terrifying as I realised she must think we were about to die! What the adults do and say around the children in a time of crisis or trauma determines how they will interpret the situation! Children need to feel that the adults are in control because if they aren't then they become terrified. In one of their bestselling books on trauma, Dr Peter Levine and Maggie Kline (2017) sum this up perfectly:

> Children take more from their feelings of their parents than from their words. Their needs have less to do with information and more with security. Children need to know they are protected and loved… (p.429)

We do know that if the adult's face showed terror at the time of a crisis or shock, any negative impact of that can be undone later on by the adult chatting gently to the child about their reaction and what was happening, whilst reassuring them. This can model self-awareness and processing emotional reactions as a normal part of life and also decreases the child's anxiety about the experience.

Sharing the experience of trauma

When we are thinking about collective trauma, the adults involved are usually as submerged in the trauma as the younger people, if not more, and yet only sometimes do they feel equipped and ready to help navigate others through that which they themselves also feel so overwhelmed by. However, we know that when the parents and carers understand the impact of trauma and realise how important their role is, they can feel equipped and empowered to make a difference to lives around them, despite their own distress. In fact, although it demands emotional energy and strength to support others when we are ourselves feeling overwhelmed, it can be life changing in its benefit to both the children and ourselves as we work to navigate the children through the collective trauma. The most extraordinary power of the primary caregiver has been evidenced in different research which is mind blowing and yet rarely shared with parents and carers. Alexander McFarlane, who researches trauma and how people react to different community traumas, reported that studies after World War II evidenced the impact of the adult's facial reaction in a crisis:

> Following World War II, studies found that the level of upset displayed by the adult in a child's life, not the war itself, was the single most important factor in predicting the emotional well being and recovery of the child. (1988, n.p.)

In fact, a 1943 study by Anna Freud and Dorothy Burlingham (pioneering child psychoanalysts who were early researchers in the field of children's mental health) showed that those children who stayed in the bombed cities, despite the level of fear, were less traumatised than those who went to the countryside to safety (Brom, Pat-Horenczyk and Ford 2009, p.72).

Parents need support themselves

When parents feel supported, listened to, valued and trusted, they can show more resilience and also be a protector in their child's life. If they are supported, cared for, listened to and feel emotionally safe then they are more able to be a support to their children. When there are cultures of shame and blame around parenting, parents may take longer to trust other adults and be honest about their difficulties and so the journey to a family being strengthened can take longer. Shame and blame are the opposite of a trauma-informed approach. Research has evidenced that 'the presence of social support for primary caregivers is a very important protective fact while the lack of it is a risk factor for the development of adult PTSD' (Brom *et al.* 2009, p.53). Caring for the children and young people without giving time and space to their adult caregivers make little sense in the long term. Ideally, we need those adult carers to be able to support their young people and build healthy long-term relationships with them.

What do I do when I am more overwhelmed and upset than they are?

This can often be the situation and the adults need to know that trying to find their own relational connections in a traumatic time is so important and not at all selfish. When an adult experiences support and they are not isolated or ignored then they feel more able to keep offering the children the nurture and attention that they need.

Often, when everything seems overwhelming and it is difficult to work out what to focus on and how to help their children, the best thing parents and carers can ask is 'I am wondering what the biggest worry is that you have right now?' because we can often be surprised about what they need to know. It is important to protect them from some detail or some of the more traumatic information according to their age and understanding, and sometimes as adults we need to ask others for help in working out what needs to be said and when, because it can be hard for us to see things subjectively.

We can often think that we need to give complex answers to their questions about complicated situations when actually the child is concerned about the welfare of their cat and if it still has the toy that they gave them for their birthday. As a mum I have so often nearly completely misfired in conversation with my children because I guessed what questions they needed answers to! Other useful questions can be:

- What could make you feel safe right now?

- What could we do that would make you feel a bit better just today?

Sometimes it is the littlest things that make the biggest difference

It can seem silly and almost seem to devalue the reality of the traumatic experience, but the smallest things can take the sting and terror away from some terrifying situations. For example, there was a time when my fourth son was taken suddenly into intensive care in hospital – he was struggling to breathe and we really thought he might die. My other three children were being looked after in the waiting area. They all knew the severity of the situation but, whilst getting themselves some food and drink from the vending machine, they found themselves searching for coins under the large machine. My eldest three sons are now adults and still talk about how they were immersed in the distraction of finding these coins for several hours, which took a great amount of the immediate terror and worry away. I am still grateful for those coins and wonder if someone was rolling them there purely to benefit my children. Distraction in the short term can be of great benefit and doesn't devalue the enormity of the situation.

With all traumatic experiences and all collective trauma experiences, the child will measure how safe they are and how bad the situation is by looking at the face of their primary attachment figure or adult looking after them. If they look terrified, the child will probably experience terror, but if the primary caregiver is able to reassure and comfort, then the child may be able to be unaware of the severity of the situation.

Upskilling parents and other adults should be a priority

Parents need to be taught about the impact of trauma and the themes that occur when people experience bereavement or loss. When they have the language to use and confidence that what they are doing lessens the negative impact both long term and short term, then they feel less panicky and stressed too.

It is normal for children to need reassurance and comfort when they feel afraid, but when the fear is severe and accompanied by a sense of powerlessness, then the child is going to need the adult to help them feel safe and empowered. When parents and carers understand the difference, they can provide the help that is needed to minimise long-term negative impact.

Offering sensory comfort and support

Sensory comfort is a powerful help to bring calm in a chaotic world or season of life. It is important to grasp how normal it is for children and young people to show regressive behaviour and be more clingy, needy and attention seeking when they feel unsafe. Remember that attention seeking is really attachment seeking – they are showing us that they need relationship with us as adults! We can often see primitive reactions to fear – wetting themselves, struggling to use words, struggling to listen well or articulate much, screamy, aggressive, angry, tantrums and other behaviours. The behaviours are a demonstration that they are trying to be okay, but are struggling and need additional support from the adults who care for them.

Parents have the ability to use touch in a way that creates comfort. Skin on skin at the point of birth is becoming more popular because we know it can help with bonding. Premature babies thrive when they have skin contact. The skin is the largest sense organ and it can feel comforting and reassuring to have a hug, massage or even a back scratch! The use of touch, when initiated by the child, with clear boundaries of respect around their bodies and never inappropriately or with persuasion of any kind, can facilitate a feeling of calm, safety and nurture.

Two dysfunctional patterns to watch for

Sometimes, when collective trauma overwhelms everyone, there can be some familiar coping patterns appearing which are damaging to family relationships. One is scapegoating, which is when everyone blames one person or projects onto them all the painful feelings they are feeling. Sometimes the child themself internalises all the responsibility, blame and shame for what has happened because the adult who should be caring for them is overwhelmed and self-focused. The other unhealthy coping mechanism is when the children realise how traumatised their adults are and so swap roles with them and take on the role of carer. People often say things like, 'they are old and responsible for their age', but actually they have lost a sense of the innocence of childhood and don't experience the power of being protected.

Traditions and rituals

Families and communities often have traditions that enable people to feel a sense of belonging and can affirm their collective identity. It could be birthdays, holiday traditions, family meals, traditional celebrations or simple things like playing a game with a certain snack. All these seemingly small things become much more important when life is uncertain and when sadness is a theme. It can take emotional courage to keep doing them, especially if life feels so different to before the collective trauma; however, these things can bring a sense of belonging, community, togetherness and a taste of normal – even if there are gaping holes where people or buildings or things used to be. Some people feel like it would be inappropriate, disloyal or disrespectful to continue to engage in family or community celebrations or rituals, but actually they help bring about a sense of hope in the midst of the loss, sadness, isolation and shock. Sometimes, creating new traditions or rituals can be helpful so that there is a sense of the future and some signposts to look for in the journey of life.

Reflection points

- How can we support other adults? What is stopping us?

- What can we do as adults when we feel totally overwhelmed but we need to care for children?

- What traditions or rituals do you now appreciate and can you keep going forward? Are there any new ones you could start?

Chapter Six

BIG STRONG EMOTIONS

Most of us remember the moment we were told about something devastating or shocking. Maybe you remember when a loved one announced they had a severe illness or when it was announced that Princess Diana had died in a car crash or when you heard about 9/11. Many of us can remember the initial emotions that hit us and then often our memories are more like slow motion, as the details of what we did next are overcome by the emotions that shook our whole being. Our initial emotional reaction is often connected to the feeling of shock and overwhelm, and then we often go through a myriad of other emotions and feelings.

The feeling of overwhelming shock

The experience of shock can cause people to feel frightened as they question their initial reactions. It is not abnormal for a person who is suddenly shocked by something like bad news or the sound of a crash or gunshot to scream, or scream internally but make no sound, or wet themselves, or cry, or struggle to breathe and describe it as if a heavy cloud came over them. Some people describe the moment as the time they ran, or they curled up in a ball and sobbed whilst others gasped and froze on the spot while time stood still.

There are so many reactions to shock and all are 'normal'. Usually the person's subsequent actions or behaviour become blurred in some way. Ideally there would be someone there to help the person breathe, feel safe and supported and less alone.

In an ideal situation, the child hearing any bad news would have an adult there to support them. Obviously, this is not always the case, and very often the people who may be with the child could be as shocked and terrified as the child. In this case, it is preferable for another adult to be there to direct the shocked people into a place of safety, such as suggesting they sit down, offering some physical reassurance like holding their hand or offering a hug for them to cry into and then finding some further sensory comfort for them, such as a cup of tea for the adult and a teddy for the child.

Repressing emotions

For many people, that initial shock begins a journey of many emotions that can seem out of control and can seem to dominate their daily life. This can often lead to both adults and children preferring to repress the emotions that seem to be hindering them. This is a protective mechanism which seeks to reduce the intensity of daily life to be manageable. Sometimes we can try to mentally interpret and analyze our feelings rather than feel them, because that feels too disruptive and uncontrollable. But where do all those feelings of terror, overwhelm, anger, rage, frustration, sadness and devastation disappear to? Of course, we know that they haven't disappeared but instead reveal their existence in behaviour, sleeplessness, physical illness and other ways. The emotions need expressing in a way that feels safe and where the person doesn't have to feel powerless to the process.

Often cultures that heavily value cognitive approaches to life and devalue emotions can make us feel that it is better to hide our real emotions, maybe try harder to cope or 'be brave' and get on with things, pretending we are 'fine'. We know that in the short term repressing our feelings is a survival response, but in the long term it can be destructive. Yet our culture can sometimes encourage secrecy and avoidance of expressing strong or difficult emotions as we lack understanding of how to sit alongside those difficult feelings. This contrasts with other cultures who confidently express deep grief when losing a loved one, with shared weeping and wailing. Trauma specialist, Karen Treisman also makes this point, stating:

> …Trauma is often invisible, missed, camouflaged, overlooked, invalidated, or unknown; and also, is often interlinked with shame, secrecy, avoidance, and silence. (2021, p.62)

Using language around trauma and shock

Helping children to put their feelings into words is of vital importance. Dan Siegel, a clinical professor of psychiatry, and Tina Payne Bryson, a clinical social worker, are best-selling authors of books about children and young people and wellbeing. They have a strategy called 'Name it to Tame it', which explains the power of naming the emotion we are feeling and helping the children we are supporting name it too. These authors explore the impact of helping a child name their emotion, to enable them to be less overwhelmed by the experience of it. The suggestion is that we can narrate, like a story, what we think the child may be feeling, by talking about how our bodies can feel when we experience an emotion. When we do this, the child becomes less scared and overwhelmed as they hear our empathetic description and validation of how they may be feeling. For example, I would say something like, 'Oh goodness I am feeling a little nervous about going home and I can feel my tummy is bubbly and my head feels a little dizzy. I know I will be okay, but I think I am scared something will surprise me again. I will do my special breathing now to calm myself.'

There are other ways to help children explore their emotions such as using picture boards and books with descriptive words around emotions, which can be chatted through with the adult.

Self-regulation and co-regulation

Children are dependent on adults to self-regulate. Ideally in the first five years of life, the child will learn to self-regulate because of the repetitive, consistent experience of co-regulation with the attentive, nurturing parent or carer. Co-regulation is the experience of the caring adult being present when a child is having an emotional reaction. Whilst offering comfort, kindness and attention, the adult validates the feelings that the child may be having and simultaneously offers a solution – either a distraction or a resolution. When this is repeated often enough, the child learns language around their emotions but also learns some skills of how to manage the strong reactions.

When the child knows that they won't be left alone to cope with their strong feelings, but will have help and support from a trusted adult, they are moved from a place of survival into a place of being able to learn and then reflect. Without adults being consistently emotionally available, traumatised children will not be able to have any sense of hope for their future because they are still trying to survive and fight to stay alive in the present.

Emotions that get stuck in the body

When any of us have experienced fight, flight or freeze in reaction to the experience of trauma, our bodies need to complete the process, because these responses can cause the body to store the nervous energy which needs to be discharged. Bessel van der Kolk, who has discovered much about the impact of trauma on the body, says:

Trauma is remembered not as a story; a narrative with a beginning middle and an end, but as isolated sensory imprints: images, sounds, and physical sensations that are accompanied by intense emotions, usually terror and helplessness. (van der Kolk 2014, p.70)

The first step to allowing the body to recover from trauma is to recognise where it is holding onto unexpressed emotions and physical memories. For example, I have had a number of children as clients who have needed to run out of school because their flight response was never completed having wanted to run from abusers. In therapy we were able to facilitate that completion in a profound and moving way, and the children didn't need to run anymore. Their instinctive running at school was never as a result of a thought through response to anything, but was a physiological, instinctive reaction to experiences of terror, shame and powerlessness that in their subconscious reminded them of the abuse. Other activities that can work to release the trapped energy are things like exercise and breathing exercises.

Anxiety and worry

Many children may experience anxiety and worry which can then impact their sleep and behaviour. Obviously, this is a normal reaction to an abnormal situation. There are some things that we adults can do to help them:

- Giving words to the feelings around worry and anxiety whilst validating them and reassuring them that it is normal in these difficult circumstances.

- Try to make a regular space to enable the child to talk

about their worries. Although bedtime seems the obvious time, this can then impact their sleep because there is less time for them to process the conversation.

- If the child struggles to talk about their worries, they can have a teddy or a worry monster or a worry box to put any worries in so that the adult can find them and initiate the chat. Initiating the conversation about worries can often be the biggest anxiety for a child, because they don't want to be inconvenient or cause their adult more stress.

- Teaching a child breathing exercises and relaxation exercises is a life-long skill that will benefit them long term. It is best for them to do it one to one rather than in a group while they learn the skills, because these activities could be triggering or uncomfortable and the child may need reassurance and support.

Emotions can be very overwhelming, frightening and cause children to feel powerless and nervous about their internal state. They need the support of adults to help them explore, recognise, name and express their emotions so that they can move on. Adults can also experience the same strong emotions and, in the same way, they need other adults to support them and comfort them and enable them to feel safe enough to talk about and express emotions, including ones that have become stuck in the body.

Reflection points

- What are the most difficult emotions that children need to express when they have been traumatised?

- What culture is there in your family around the expression of emotions? Are there any less acceptable emotions?

- How can we as the adults provide safety for the child to explore their emotions?

Chapter Seven

CREATIVE IDEAS AND ACTIVITIES TO HELP

We recognise that trying to talk about traumatic experiences can be sometimes limiting, sometimes difficult, sometimes impossible or at worst re-traumatising; and so to facilitate recovery, we are dependent on creative activities to use with children to help reduce their turmoil, emotional pain, numbness and overwhelm.

The power of play

Play is the main language that children use to learn and interact with the world. The whole concept of allowing children time to play because they have earned it after working hard is ridiculous, because play is hard work to a child who seeks to learn about and discover their world. When adults can provide materials and inspire them to play, they will be stimulated, practise relational skills, use their imaginations and make sense of their world. They don't even need toys and can happily use natural things like sticks, bricks or stones, cloth and boxes or random items that can be found. Children can naturally 'play out' their worries and curiosity about their experiences whilst enjoying the company of others.

Post-traumatic play is a term to describe the play of children who have experienced single incident trauma, where the play is based on both the recurring memories and the re-enactment of the event. Lenore Terr, a psychiatrist and childhood trauma specialist, first used the term (1991) to describe the play activity of children who have experienced traumatic events but not had sufficient resolution of the emotions associated with the events. 'In contrast to normal play, which leads to pleasure, satisfying expression, problem solving and learning, posttraumatic play is often anxiety ridden and constricted, repetitive, rigid, and without resolution' (Malchiodi 2008, p.33). In such play, there needs to be adults present, unobtrusively, helping the children explore resolution, hope and being able to 'contain' the strong memories that need externalising in this way. Of course, one idea is to have a hero in every story told, who the children look for or choose to act out. This person is the helper, the kind person, the one we need to train ourselves to look out for when the world feels full of horror and darkness.

It is important to remember that any toys that are used need to express a sense of diversity with thought-through cultural sensitivity, so that the children can identify with them, rather than feel excluded and different. If the toys all represent a different culture to the child's own, then the play won't be able to facilitate proper processing, but could cause further internal distress that may not be shown.

Sensory exploration

When people have experienced trauma, they can have heightened sensitivity to sensory stimulation. In order to try to protect themselves from any further terror, they stay on alert for any signals of danger and this means that they can be hypervigilant to sounds, smells, sights, touch and feelings. This can mean that their sensory system is easily overwhelmed, which leads to difficulty with processing sensory information. Therefore, it can be helpful for children to be allowed to explore different sensory experiences and for them to see which are helpful and pleasurable and learn to interact with them, without being overwhelmed. They can rip newspaper and throw it or soak it in water and throw it against a wall. They can use paints and feel the soft brushes before they have paint on and then feel the paint with their hands. They can smell the playdough and squish the clay. They can shake glitter and watch it go everywhere and bang the drums and make other loud sounds. When they feel in control of these experiences, they can experiment and build up their tolerance for sensory stimulation which, at the same time, decreases the overwhelm of stored sensory memories that contain turmoil and pain.

Having explored the use of sensory play with freedom to experiment, it is worth noting again that boundaries are important and helping the child feel safe is vital. For example, clay is often triggering for those who have been sexually abused and the sound of the thud of newspaper being thrown against a wall could be deeply triggering for someone who has heard or seen people being hurt physically with a sound of a similar thud. There always needs to be a sense of respect, empathy and curiosity to which sounds or feelings could trigger a sensory memory and what would happen if it did? Is there a safe place for them to go to? Is this the right time for them to explore this or do they need some more time to build relationship or stabilise their home life first? We shouldn't use sensory play without thought and reflection as a team around the child first, so that we can avoid any obvious triggers and prepare a safe place if they get overwhelmed.

Storytelling

Stories can be vital to help a child explore what has happened, what could happen or what has happened to others without it being intense or overwhelming. There are many fantastic therapeutic story books available that explore traumatic experiences subtly, within the framework of the story being about an animal or another child. This helps them know that they are not the only one who has experienced this trauma, helps them feel less shame and thus enables them to be more able to speak about their experience. The story can answer some of their questions and also gives the adult a chance to ask the child questions, such as 'who do you like in the book?' and 'are you like any of the characters in the story?'

They can be asked if they would like to rewrite the ending of the story and if they would add or take away any aspect of the story. These questions can help us understand more of what the child needs and help them process some of what has happened to them. Stories stimulate both hemispheres of the brain, which strengthens their brain and creates more integration and therefore wholeness. When listening to a story, the right hemisphere of the brain is often stimulated with an emotional reaction to what happens to the character in the story at the same time as the left hemisphere of the brain is stimulated by being curious, reflecting and being empathetic to the character. Some therapeutic stories can explore themes of survival, hope, resilience, courage, loss, fear, strength, future dreams and many other important themes alongside giving images to help children picture experiences such as funerals, hospital visits, and events like the first day back somewhere after a difficult time.

Adults can also find storytelling particularly helpful to express some of their experiences and feelings around the collective trauma experience, either by writing, drawing, cartooning or telling the story to others who are empathetic, kind and listen with respect.

Music

Making music is a powerful method to enable people of all ages to express emotions at the same time as building a sense of community and belonging. Playing and making music is emotive and can immediately change a person's mood. It can be really important to help children and young people to explore what they like and what is unhelpful for them so that they can use music to comfort, calm or motivate them.

Drumming is also a helpful way of expressing emotion and simple drumming or clapping can be facilitated by anyone to great effect. Group drumming can be a powerful way to enable a sense of belonging, especially when it is led by someone who can encourage participation and confidence with their leading. Call and response games are always profound ways to build relationship because the child experiences the feeling of being listened to and copied when they hear their rhythm played back, which boosts confidence and trust. Singing songs together can facilitate a sense of belonging and also release the feel-good hormones of serotonin and endorphins, whilst writing songs can help find words to express feelings and experiences.

Using art

When working with children who are traumatised, it is important to recognise that art and creative materials need to be used with careful planning, because some sensory experiences can be triggering and cause an explosion of non-verbal or subconscious memories to surface which could overwhelm the person. When using creative materials, the activities need to offer some sense of containment and safety to avoid the person inadvertently expressing and exploring too large an issue before they are ready. The pace of expression and exploration is central to safe processing. This is why qualified art and music psychotherapists take so many years to train – to learn the skills to provide the safety. Any activity used with people who have experienced significant trauma need to have been thought through to facilitate boundaries and safety. For children who have been exposed to a collective trauma experience who have had enough support and where their losses have not been devastating, there are far fewer concerns around the safety of using creative tools. Whatever the background of the adult helping, it is important to be attuned and observing, reflecting and evaluating the use of the sensory, creative materials in order to make sure they are soothing and not triggering or causing feelings of confusion, 'stuck-ness' or pressure. When there is recognition of the strength of the creative activities to powerfully unlock our internal processes, there can be a healthy respect for the process.

The creative arts are helpful for enabling emotions to be expressed and to reveal what is really being felt beneath the defence mechanisms that exist to protect the vulnerable self. Malchiodi explains that 'Art expression helps to resist and protest what has occurred. Art consoles and gives voice to the philosophical, political and spiritual questions' (2008, p.83).

Creative ideas

- Create a safe place for a toy pet. This home or safe place can be made out of clay, junk, card or anything else and the child can add what they see as other essentials for them to feel safe. This helps the child explore in the metaphor what they need to help them feel safe and also helps the adult then identify if those needs can be facilitated for them.

- Mask making, where the child can paint the inside of the mask with how they feel and the outside with how people see them. This can help the child explore these important issues in the context of a warm and kind adult who helps reassure them and can reflect with them if they want to make any changes. Again, this needs to be done within the context of a therapeutic relationship which has regular arranged times for sessions, where there is safety in knowing that the exploration can continue and is safe in the hands of or to be witnessed by this person they can trust.

- Blowing bubbles and playing blow football can really help to practice breathing in a playful way that can also build relationship.

- Make a poster to help other children who have experienced the collective trauma with what has helped them. This enables the child to feel less powerless and helps them realise how many skills they have and what they have learned.

- Create a shield out of card to ask, 'What makes you feel protected? Powerful? What are you good at? What would we say about you?' This brings clarity and confidence to a child who feels like everything has gone wrong and they are completely powerless.

- Sit in a circle with each person holding a drum and one at a time a person plays a simple rhythm and the others copy. The rhythms could be put together as a whole piece. It is fun and everyone feels listened to and part of a group.

- Splashing paint or water on large spaces can be playful, fun and releasing. Doing it with others can build a sense of community and belonging.

There are loads of other ideas which can be found in the recommended reading at the back of this book, but I hope that this gives a taste of the kind of things that can help children and young people express emotions, explore their reactions and experiences and feel listened to, valued and heard.

Reflection points

- With the children you are caring for, does play, sensory play, music or art hold their interest the most?

- Have you found that a child has been triggered by an activity? How did you notice? How did you support and reassure them and enable them to feel safe?

- What activities have you done with children who have experienced collective trauma? Why do you think they worked so well?

Chapter Eight

GRIEF, LOSS AND BEREAVEMENT

Being human, we are all impacted by loss and grief at some point in our lives. The experience of collective trauma involves some aspect of loss. It could be the loss of routine, loss of familiarity, loss of innocence, loss of freedom, loss of simplicity or it could be the loss of a regular income, a home, family member or friend. Loss touches everyone in some way and so this chapter will explore some of the key issues.

Questions around death

It is essential that we recognise that children have many questions about death and dying and it is important that we take time to help them understand. If the collective trauma experience has involved significant loss of life, then it is essential that we have language around death, including clarity about where someone is when they are late or not around due to house moves or job changes, etc. Children can begin to assume that anyone who is not there when they usually are is probably dead and so it's important to always be clear about where people are. Even if a family hasn't experienced a death in the family, any illness can become a source of anxiety because the link between death and illness can be confusing for them.

It's also important to always remember child development stages so that we can recognise what a child or young person may understand or need to know at what age. Young children may struggle to grasp the permanency of death and assume the person will come back, and so it is important to gently try to explain that. Young children are naturally egocentric due to their developmental age and therefore they can sometimes think it's their fault that the person died, because of something they did before the death. Obviously, it is important to make sure the child has space and time to be reassured that they are not responsible and then ask any questions that may be troubling them.

How to talk about death

It is important that we check out each child's family and cultural perspective on death and what they believe happens and think carefully about the language that we may find normal around the subject. The concept of 'passing on' or 'passing away' is a very abstract one for a child who may assume the person who they are speaking about may have passed on to a new job, house or a holiday. When adults talk about death using words that are associated with sleep, children can often become scared of sleep and think that they may 'pass away' and not come back to those they love. Language can be very confusing for children and so it is best to be honest and answer questions sensitively, carefully but honestly and at an age-appropriate level.

The grieving process

It is important to recognise that everyone handles loss and death differently and there are no 'right' ways. Some children may cry more or be withdrawn or sad, whilst others may want to act normally or act out a little bit with fidgeting or agitation, and some may need more comfort and reassurance, or they may need to run and move more.

There are social expectations for adults of how we should grieve and how we should be feeling, whereas children don't have those preconceptions. Sometimes children don't react in ways we think they should and instead they carry on behaving in ways that are appropriate to their age with giggling, screaming or playing. They can seem oblivious to any tragedy and this can seem inappropriate at times, such as when a family are crying or the funeral. Some adults would expect the child to look sad and serious, but we know that the child will grow in their understanding of death and they may be unlikely to have fully understood it despite the public expectation of what is appropriate behaviour.

Before a child can in any way begin to grieve the loss of a loved one, they need to feel safe. For some children that means that they need to firstly have a sense of future confidence about their home, other family and friends, school, hobbies and what else will change. Malchiodi (2008) says that '…establishing safety and instilling the inner strength to modify overwhelming emotions and memories produced by the trauma was necessary before grief work could begin' (p.109).

Themes in grief

When a child experiences some kind of loss there could be a whole host of other emotional issues that become themes for them, such as blaming themselves, abandonment, guilt that they did or didn't do something, confusion about what happened, fear of losing others, feelings of betrayal and anger, becoming the carer of siblings or parents, powerlessness and, of course, anger, sadness and shame. It's important to know with each child what themes are surfacing alongside the loss, so that they can express any emotions and find comfort in our response. We have to offer comfort, validate any emotions and try to answer any questions that they may ask.

A lot of children will keep their feelings inside if they think that it will upset others. They may 'press down' their grief and turmoil to act as normal as possible so that they can support their remaining family or not distract from the person that has died. Every time a child keeps their feelings inside, they can then feel lonely because when they push their feelings down, they have to withdraw so that people don't see what is lurking beneath the surface of their forced smiles. Therefore, it is important to create safe spaces for anyone who has had someone close to them die so that they can take time to slowly explore their feelings, with no rush, judgement or sense that they will be an inconvenience.

It is also important to remember that some adolescents process their anger around death by an increase in risky behaviour. This seems to also be a way to show themselves that they are not scared of death and so death has no power over them.

The impact of grief

It is easy to recognise that grief can make us feel sad or depressed, but there are also physical aspects of grieving. Grief can cause us humans to feel disconnected from our every day, to feel different from those who complain at tiny little matters, it can cause brain fog and can also have a negative impact on our confidence. Some people seem to need to be public grievers and talk and be with others who have also experienced grief, and others find solace in activities such as gardening or exercise. Grief doesn't have to cause trauma (a sense of terror, powerlessness and overwhelm) if those around the grieving person make space for them to take the time to get over the shock and then reorganise their lives in the light of their loss.

Some important aspects of the bereavement process

Rando (1993) has identified some aspects of bereavement which seem to be familiar for those who have had someone they love die. He calls them the six Rs of bereavement and he suggests that people all need to have explored these areas. He says that we will have times where we need to Recognise the loss and times where we will React to the separation of the one who has died. We will then find that we will spend time Recollecting the person we miss and our relationships with them, whilst Relinquishing and Readjusting to life without them. Finally we need to Reinvent ourselves emotionally as we invest into other people and things in our present life.

Another grief framework is by Dr Robert Neimeyer (2012) who speaks about making meaning after we have lost a loved one. He calls his framework 'The Three R's of Processing Grief' and speaks of the need to Retell our story constantly until the story changes. He also highlights the importance of Rebuilding the bond with the person who has died through working out how to conserve the connection of love with them. The third R represents the need to Reinvent our lives and ourselves knowing that we are not the same but need to move forward holding hope and sadness.

What can we do to help the grieving?

There are some practical activities that we can do to help the grieving child.

- We can help them make memory boxes which contain special memories of the loved one – photos, a scarf, a book, a special object that has meaning to the child.

- We can also help them make safety boxes with objects in the box that help the child feel a sense of comfort and safety. This can have sensory items within it (things that smell good, feel good, sound good or taste good) and photos of happy times.

- We can help them to retell any aspect of their story of what happened in creative ways. As we have already said, using words can be too overwhelming, but exploring aspects of the story in drawings, writings, dolls house, puppets and story boards can enable them to experiment themselves with what they can tolerate and what is too much for now.

- We also need to help them limit what they read or view on screens about any collective trauma. Sometimes the child may become obsessed with the matter, because it can be a way of feeling close to their loved one who has died.

Survivor's guilt

Those who survived did just that – they survived – and yet some struggle to fully live because of the weight of guilt that they survived when so many others didn't. This issue is another one that relies on others to help the person navigate, because isolation can feed the negative thought patterns that lead to overwhelming guilt and shame. Sometimes those who stayed alive become fearful of death or further disaster and become reticent to take risks. Sometimes comparison can become a pattern, where children compare their pain to another and then feel shame about the weight of negative feelings they have. In the context of empathetic, kind, patient adults, the child will be able to explore these feelings and thoughts and move through them into freedom from them.

Our own journey

As we conclude this overview of the important issue of grief and loss, it is important that we recognise that, as the adults caring for the children, we have to tap into our own grief in order to be empathetic and caring and that can be painful for us. We need the support of others who recognise that loss can impact us long term and that whilst the pain can lesson over time and with the support of empathic people around us, it is still a natural part of what makes us human and therefore doesn't just disappear.

Reflection points

- Are you aware of how your cultural traditions around death differ from other cultures?

- What questions would you be fearful of answering?

- What have you found comforting and helpful when you have experienced loss?

Chapter Nine

A TRAUMA-INFORMED AND RECOVERY-FOCUSED CULTURE

Cultural diversity and humility

Collective trauma impacts every culture in some way and so central to understanding its impact is the understanding of cultural diversity. Our cultural background is one of many different cultures which are present in the world today. An important aspect of empathy is the ability to 'stand in the shoes of another' and learn what it would be like to be them. This can only take place when we firstly understand the importance of being culturally competent and culturally humble. Culturally competent is when we as humans value gaining factual knowledge about other people and their culture and communities, so that we can avoid assumptions or generalisations. Cultural humility is a vital approach, in which we choose to have a humble and respectful attitude towards everyone from all different cultures.

Hook and colleagues (2013) conceptualise cultural humility as the 'ability to maintain an interpersonal stance that is other-oriented (or open to the other) in relation to aspects of cultural identity that are most important to the [person]' (p.354).

Cultural humility starts as an attitude and approach to others, but then leads to some actions. First, we are people who are self-aware of our own histories and experiences and recognise that we will have some subconscious bias due to them. When we can be humble and self-reflective, we can seek to learn and grow and through learning and curiosity can change our perception of others.

Cultural humility also recognises that power imbalances exist and subconscious bias exists which can cause devaluing or discrimination. Cultural humility is a commitment to being intentional to bring about change so that powerlessness and domination are no longer a reality or fear.

An exploration of culture

The culture of a group of people is shaped by its values, beliefs, traditions and shared experiences; these may be different to those of another culture. Culture is learned and shared by the people who live in the same environment. In a family, the culture is shaped by the parents or adults leading this micro-organisation to become the community that they had planned, according to their own cultures, ideals, values, vision and beliefs and then of course, their ability to bring that about. For example, poverty could hinder the outworking of their values and vision for their family by stopping them enjoying shared meals due to having to work long hours or by not having the funds to buy enough food to share easily. Some families are not intentional about creating the culture of their family and have just accepted the cultures that they grew up in and automatically continue to outwork them.

In an organisation, the leader or leadership team are able to set the cultural expectations of the workplace, by clearly communicating them before people enrol onto the staff and then continuing to communicate them as they share their common work objectives together. Other larger communities also have clearly communicated cultural values and also share historic experiences from their own life or generations before them. There are aspects of cultures that can be evident externally in clothing or behaviour and aspects that are more internal, such as attitude, belief and philosophical values. Every community and organisation has a certain culture, but some are intentional and planned and others have instead been formed naturally over time, due to experiences and their reactions to them. Communities that value trauma-informed principles and have intentionally embedded them into their culture can have greater resilience when they experience collective trauma.

There are organisations that have written their cultural values which may contain trauma-informed principles, but they seem unable to outwork them into their day to day work life. This could be due to division amongst the people in that community, or due to lack of strong leadership, or lack of finance to fulfil their aims, or due to a lack of understanding of the power of trauma-informed living. Collective trauma can impact a culture and bring about change to beliefs, values and practice; in these instances there needs to be clarity, leadership and an intentional focus on practices that recognise and strengthen the power of positive relationships to facilitate wellbeing. Trauma-informed practice and principles need to guide and influence a community in order for it to recover and grow from the traumatic experience rather than suffer collectively and become saturated in hopelessness.

Trauma-informed culture

A trauma-informed culture is one that enables individuals and communities to feel safe when they have experienced collective or individual trauma or any other adversity. Safety is the foundation to recovery. Culture takes time to create – it is not achieved in a day's training or a policy, rather it is a way of living that others notice. It's the day to day experience that is shared by everyone.

The beliefs that shape a trauma-informed culture are:

- We recognise the impact of trauma and can identify trauma symptoms.

- We believe that 'behaviour is communication' and so we are curious about what the child's behaviour is telling us rather than assuming that they are naughty.

- We know that fear causes protective, defensive behaviours that sometimes can be problematic to others and when we can help the child or adult feel listened to, cared for and valued, the fear can decrease.

- We recognise that children need adults to care, protect, nurture, teach, help and co-regulate their emotions with them. We know that co-regulation is a pre-requisite to self-regulation.

- We know how powerful attachment relationships can be. Children need to have one or more important long-term relationship, where the adult is attuned, consistent, predictable and emotionally available. We need to support these attachment relationships.

- We know that emotions can be powerful and scary for those children who have been traumatised and that they need help to name the emotions and express them in a way that is not damaging.

- We know that safety is critical for recovery and as such we are intentional about creating emotionally safe places for the children and adults.

- Kindness, compassion, empathy and nurture are the core values.

The Betsy de Thierry Trauma Recovery-Focused Approach (2016) that I use in my clinical practice builds on these foundations but goes on to add:

- A recognition that a thorough trauma assessment is important to know how severe the impact of trauma has been to each individual and therefore what recovery plan is appropriate.

- The subconscious is recognised as holding the implicit, sensory memories of trauma and this influences behaviour, thinking and safety.

- Each child who has experienced complex trauma needs help to process their subconscious through skilled, trained help.

- The child needs to have any different professionals helping them working well together in a culture of trust and respect.

- Recovery is possible and we will hold that hope for the child until they can believe it too.

Re-traumatisation

A child, family, adult or staff member of an organisation can become re-traumatised if the trauma-informed culture is not naturally part of the lived practice of the community. For example we know that trauma can be defined as an experience where the person is terrified, powerless and overwhelmed, and so when our collective response to a traumatic experience causes people to feel further terrified or powerless or unable to understand what is going on – and therefore overwhelmed – the person may feel further traumatised. We know that we need to aim to always make sure that fear is decreased by being kind, caring, thoughtful and emotionally available. We know that when people feel powerless that they can feel fear escalate due to past experiences of powerlessness when they were hurt. Therefore, it is important to make time to listen to people, empower them to help find solutions and make sure that they are not ignored, left out or depowered.

Compassion, kindness and empathy

A trauma-informed organisation or person is human focused. We recognise the frailty, strength and needs of all humans and recognise how to create cultures where people can have a sense of belonging and purpose and where they are valued as individuals with skills and strengths to share and weaknesses that need supporting.

Reflection points

- Could you describe your cultural background and what values you hold as important?

- How is the family, organisation or community expressing their cultural values and in what ways are they trauma-informed?

- What are your most important values for your personal life?

Chapter Ten

BUILDING FOR THE FUTURE, RESILIENCE AND POST-TRAUMATIC GROWTH

Individual resilience

There are many different definitions of resilience that people use when speaking about trauma and recovery. We often think about resilience as bouncing back from adversity or doing better than others expect when bad things have happened or having the skills to keep moving forward despite the trauma. Sometimes people who use the word seem to infer that some children are naturally 'more resilient' as if it was a personality trait, and yet others would assign the environment as the reason for a child's resilience. It is important that we understand that whilst personality types can influence our resilience, it is primarily a strength drawn from relationships. Kim Aumann and Angie Hart, who lead an organisation called BoingBoing which helps children with complex needs bounce back, define resilience as:

> The kinds of things we need to make happen (e.g. events, parenting strategies, relationships, resources) to help children manage life when it's tough. Plus ways of thinking and acting that we need ourselves if we want to make things better for children. (2009, p.11)

The important thing is to recognise that research is beginning to evidence that, as adults, we can help children develop resilience, because it is a dynamic skill that is heavily influenced by the child's relationships. Resilience in children is interconnected with how attuned and emotionally available their primary caregivers are:

> The most significant determinant of resilience – noted in nearly every review or study of resilience in the last 50 years – is the quality of our close personal relationships, especially with parents and primary caregivers. Early attachments to parents play a crucial, lifelong role in human adaptation. (Zimmerman 2020)

Three tips for developing resilience

Dr Lucy Hone (2020) gave a TEDx talk in which she described the top tips that she found helpful when she needed to develop resilience because her young daughter was suddenly killed in a car crash. She listed three helpful things to remember which can develop resilience.

- Bad things happen to almost everyone at some time. She says that we shouldn't get stuck in the place of 'why me?' but realise that most of us suffer and yet social media seems to hide it.

- Resilient people are good at choosing carefully where they select their attention. We are good at noticing negatives as humans but good experiences can bounce off us. She says that resilient people don't diminish the negative but they choose to tune into the good. Find something to be grateful for and switch our attention to what is good, even if we have to hunt for the good stuff.

- Resilient people ask themselves, 'Is what I am doing helping or harming me?' Sometimes it can be helpful to forgive people or to stop looking at social media or TV shows.

These tips explore common themes found in research about resilience. Research seems to share the similar points of being careful not to dwell on the negative, having a moral compass, having religious or spiritual beliefs, having cognitive and emotional flexibility, social connectedness and some kind of dedication to a worthy cause or a belief in something greater than oneself.

Community resilience

The term resilience is mostly used to refer to an individual child or adult. However, this doesn't take into account the social and cultural context. In this context of collective trauma, we can recognise that when the traumatic experience has been shared, it is possible for the community to develop resilience and to experience collective healing and/ or recovery. Lanau and Saul (2004) defined community resilience as 'a community's capacity, hope and faith to withstand major trauma and loss, overcome adversity and to prevail, usually with increased resources, competence and connectedness' (p.8).

The most obvious first step to building resilience in a community is a focus on enabling everyone to access their basic needs – good enough housing, enough money to buy food, being safe, access and transport, a healthy diet, exercise and fresh air, enough sleep, play and leisure, alongside living free from prejudice and discrimination. If these are difficult to provide, the community can plan strategies to enable there to be hope for them to be made a reality.

Froma Walsh, who has studied the concept of family resilience, defined resilience as 'the capacity to rebound from adversity, strengthened and more resourceful. It is an active process of endurance, self righting and growth in response to crisis and challenge...the ability to withstand and rebound from disruptive life challenges' (Walsh, quoted in Saul 2014, p.7).

For the community to recover, there needs to be time spent together with others who have shared the experience, where the collective trauma is processed, and the negative impact is validated with the aim of creating a plan for restoration. Unity is a powerful force, kindness to each other is a healing oil that soothes the pain of shared trauma and research suggests that social support may even be found to 'play a strong role in the development of posttraumatic growth when it remains stable and consistent over time' (Tedeschi and Calhoun 2004).

Cultures that support resilience

We know that some community or organisational cultures are not trauma-informed or aware, or trauma sensitive, and can actually escalate the sense of fear and powerlessness in a collective trauma. In fact, the organisations that exist to help traumatised people can become so full of staff who are now in a state of secondary trauma that there can easily be a culture of relentless hard work with little hope. When those who are in roles that are designed to bring healing and hope feel distressed and hopeless, it can cause further destruction to all involved. Often organisations become so fearful about allegations or the high demand for their work, that they can become saturated with traumatised, exhausted people, which can cause further damage to everyone. We need to build cultures that firstly respect people's needs as humans, which are centred on kindness, compassion and empathy with recognition of the frailty and strength found in our humanity.

Saul (2014) sums that up in his book, *Collective Trauma Collective Healing*:

> Major disasters that disrupt family systems, work organisations and community structures and services are most debilitating because they may lead to community fragmentation, conflict, and destabilization. Unresponsiveness by larger systems compounds the traumatic impact. (p.9)

There are some things that can help develop a resilient culture. The first and central aspect is, of course, relationships, for both adults and children. When the adults feel supported, valued and listened to, then the children are more likely to be supported in the same way.

Creativity is another key ingredient found in a culture that wants to be resilient, and some creative activities can also build a sense of belonging and community again. Play is vital for children and young people along with the learning of new skills, because that feels like an investment into the future (see Chapter 7). Animals can be helpful to bring a sense of comfort and consistency to those who spend time with them, and time spent with them can release the serotonin hormone that boosts feelings of happiness.

Post-traumatic growth

Psychologists Richard Tedeschi, PhD, and Lawrence Calhoun, PhD (2004), wrote about the way that sometimes humans can actually also experience positive elements to the recovery of their trauma, which can be referred to as post-traumatic growth. This does not deny the pain and turmoil of the traumatic experiences, but merely shows that there is research that has found that growth often co-exists with the continuing distress of the trauma. They discovered that, following a traumatic experience, children and young people can often feel more compassion and empathy for others, a deeper understanding of personal values, purpose and meaning in life; they can also place a greater value on interpersonal relationships. Also they were found to have increased psychological and emotional maturity and a more 'complex appreciation of life' compared to others of a similar age.

Their research showed that for some people, 'post traumatic growth is not simply a return to baseline – it is an experience of improvement that for some persons is deeply profound' (2004, n.p.). We know that the strongest factor in developing children's resilience and post-traumatic growth is their relationship with their primary caregivers, where they feel emotionally connected, safe and known and in this context, the collective trauma experience can be a springboard of learning and new skills which can last a lifetime.

Imagining a positive future

Imagination enables us to have hope for the future. When trauma continues to pull us back into the past, our imaginations can become stuck and so it's important to recognise the importance of imagining. Imagination can give hope, helps fire our creativity and helps us plan for enjoyable things. Malchiodi (2008) affirms this when speaking about trauma intervention: 'In trauma intervention, recalling memories of positive events that can reframe and eventually override negative ones is helpful in reducing posttraumatic stress – simple ideas like drawing a pleasant time, a familiar song or story' (p.18). It can be difficult to imagine anything positive when our brains are wired to survive and when we feel anxious about further traumatisation; however, when we can be helped to imagine something positive, beautiful or a past precious memory, we can feel hope again.

Reflection points

- What are the main ways that a child is able to develop resilience?

- What top tips will help you to be resilience minded – either from this chapter or from your life experience?

- How is post-traumatic growth possible and what could you do to facilitate it in your environment?

GLOSSARY

Attachment This word describes the crucial relationship between two people and usually refers to the relationship between a child and their primary caregiver.

Brainstem The area at the base of the brain between the spinal cord and brain hemispheres. The brainstem looks after a lot of our automatic actions such as heartbeat and breathing.

Collective trauma The reaction to an event or period of time where people share a traumatic experience whilst feeling terror, powerlessness and overwhelm. Whilst the collective trauma may be shared, the people will have varied experiences of it and will respond to these experiences differently, depending on their own personal backgrounds and current context.

Community trauma The reaction to an event or period of time where a group of people share a traumatic experience whilst feeling terror, powerlessness and overwhelm. Whilst the trauma experience may be shared by the whole group, the people will have varied experiences of it and will respond to these experiences differently, depending on their own personal backgrounds and current context.

Co-regulation Refers to the process in a relationship where one adjusts themselves when interacting with another, in order to help the other become regulated.

Fight, flight or freeze response A primitive reaction to terror and fear that is automatic and driven by the need for survival.

Primary caregiver The person whose role is to look after a baby or child and take responsibility for their needs being met as a child.

Post-traumatic stress disorder A type of anxiety disorder that may develop after being involved in, or witnessing, traumatic events.

Prefrontal cortex The part of the brain that covers the front part of the frontal lobe. This part of the brain is responsible for thinking, reflection, planning, decision making, etc.

Resilience The capacity to recover or bounce back from difficulties.

REFERENCES

Aumann, K. and Hart, A. (2009) *Helping Children with Complex Needs Bounce Back.* London: Jessica Kingsley Publishers.

Brom, D., Pat-Horenczyk, R. and Ford, J.D. (2009) *Treating Traumatized Children: Risk, Resilience and Recovery.* Hove: Routledge.

Cozolino, L. (2006) *The Neuroscience of Human Relationships: Attachment and the Developing Social Brain (Norton Series on Interpersonal Neurobiology).* New York: W.W. Norton & Company.

de Thierry, B. (2015) *Teaching the Child on the Trauma Continuum.* London: Grosvenor Publishing.

de Thierry, B. (2016) 'Trauma Recovery Focused.' Accessed on 22/02/2021 at https://www.betsytraininguk.co.uk/resources-1.

de Thierry, B. (2019) *The Simple Guide to Attachment Difficulties.* London: Jessica Kingsley Publishers.

de Thierry, B. (2020) *The Simple Guide to Complex Trauma and Dissociation.* London: Jessica Kingsley Publishers.

Erikson, K. (1986) *Everything in Its Path: Destruction of Community in the Buffalo Creek Flood.* New York: Simon & Schuster.

Freud, A. and Burlingham, D. (1943) *War and Children.* New York: Medical War Books.

Hirschberger, G. (2018) 'Collective trauma and the social construction of meaning.' *Frontiers in Psychology 9,* 1441. Accessed on 12/09/2020 at www.ncbi.nlm.nih.gov/pmc/articles/PMC6095989.

Hone, L. (2020) 'The three secrets of resilient people.' TED Talk. Accessed on 11/08/2020 at www.ted.com/talks/lucy_hone_the_three_secrets_of_resilient_people.

Hook, J.N., Davis, D.E., Owen, J., Worthington Jr, E.L. and Utsey, S.O. (2013) 'Cultural humility: Measuring openness to culturally diverse clients.' *Journal of Counseling Psychology* 60, 3, 353–366.

Lanau, J. and Saul, J. (2004) 'Facilitating family and community resilience in response to major disaster.' In F. Walsh and M. McGoldrick (eds) *Living Beyond Loss*. New York: Norton.

Levine, P. and Kline, M. (2017) *Trauma Through A Child's Eyes*. Berkeley, CA: North Atlantic Books.

McFarlane, A.C. (1988) 'The longitudinal course of posttraumatic morbidity. The range of outcomes and their predictors.' *Journal of Nervous and Mental Disease 176*, 1, 30–39.

Malchiodi, C.A. (2008) *Creative Interventions for Traumatised Children*. New York: Guilford Press.

Neimeyer, R. (2012) *Techniques of Grief Therapy: Creative Practices for Counseling the Bereaved (Series in Death, Dying, and Bereavement)*. New York: Routledge.

Porges, S. (2011) *The Polyvagal Theory: Neurophysiological Foundatons of Emotions, Attachment, Communication, and Self-Regulation*. New York: Norton.

Porges, S. (2017) *The Pocket Guide to the Polyvagal Theory*. New York: Norton.

Rando, T. (1993) *Treatment of Complicated Mourning*. Champaign, IL: Research Press.

Saul, J. (2014) *Collective Trauma Collective Healing*. New York: Routledge.

Tedeschi, R.G. and Calhoun, L.G. (2004) 'Posttraumatic growth: Conceptual foundations and empirical evidence.' *Psychological Inquiry 15*, 1, 1–18. Accessed on 07/09/2020 at https://academic.udayton.edu/jackbauer/Readings%20595/Tedeschi%2004%20PT%20growth%20copy.pdf.

Terr, L.C. (1991) 'Childhood traumas: An outline and overview.' *The American Journal of Psychiatry, 148*, 1, 10–20.

Treisman, K. (2021) *A Treasure Box for Creating Trauma-Informed Organizations: A Ready-to-Use Resource for Trauma, Adversity, and Culturally Informed, Infused and Responsive Systems.* London: Jessica Kingsley Publishers.

van der Kolk, B. (2014) *The Body Keeps The Score: Brain, Mind and Body in the Healing of Trauma.* New York: Viking, Penguin.

Young, S. (2020) 'Children likely to experience depression and anxiety post-lockdown, study says.' *The Independent,* June 1. Accessed on 12/07/2020 at www.independent.co.uk/lifestyle/health-and-families/lockdown-children-mental-health-depression-anxiety-loneliness-study-university-bath-a9541801.html.

Zimmerman, E. (2020) 'What makes some people more resilient than others.' *The New York Times,* June 18. Accessed on 16/09/2020 at www.nytimes.com/2020/06/18/health/resilience-relationships-trauma.html.

FURTHER READING

Treisman, K. (2018) *A Therapeutic Treasure Box for Working with Children and Adolescents with Developmental Trauma: Creative Techniques and Activities.* London: Jessica Kingsley Publishers.

Treisman, K. (2019a) *Binnie the Baboon Anxiety and Stress Activity Book.* London: Jessica Kingsley Publishers.

Treisman, K. (2019b) *Cleo the Crocodile Activity Book for Children Who Are Afraid to Get Close.* London: Jessica Kingsley Publishers.

Treisman, K. (2019c) *Gilly the Giraffe Self-Esteem Activity Book.* London: Jessica Kingsley Publishers.

Treisman, K. (2021) *A Treasure Box for Creating Trauma-Informed Organizations: A Ready-to-Use Resource for Trauma, Adversity, and Culturally Informed, Infused and Responsive Systems.* London: Jessica Kingsley Publishers.

van der Kolk, B. (2014) 'A revolutionary approach to treating PTSD.' *The New York Times,* May 22. Accessed on 14/09/2020 at www.nytimes.com/2014/05/25/magazine/a-revolutionary-approach-to-treating-ptsd.html?searchResultPosition=1.

INDEX